Oh You Robot Saints!

Books by Rebecca Morgan Frank

Little Murders Everywhere
The Spokes of Venus
Sometimes We're All Living in a Foreign Country
Oh You Robot Saints!

Oh You Robot Saints!

Rebecca Morgan Frank

Carnegie Mellon University Press
Pittsburgh 2021

Acknowledgments

Grateful acknowledgment is made to the following publications in which versions of these poems first appeared:

32 Poems: "Automaton Angels" and "Ode to the Water Thief"; *Academy of American Poets Poem-a-Day*: "Not Everybody's Bestiary (Yet)"; *American Poetry Review*: "Self-Operating Machines"; *Beloit Poetry Journal*: "Claqueurs"; *Bennington Review*: "Invention #4"; *The Common*: "I hold with those who favor fire"; *Diode*: "Creation" and "Loving the dead is what we are here for"; *The Florida Review*: "Gerbert of Aurillac and the Magic 8 Ball"; *The Kenyon Review*: "A Field Guide to Mythological Botany" and "Epithalamion Aubade"; *Miracle Monocl*: "Vaucanson's Digesting Duck Automaton, c. 1739"; *The New Yorker*: part one of "The Girlfriend Elegies"; *Nimrod*: "Monk Automaton, c. 1560"; *On the Seawall*: "The Fool of Aljaferia Palace Encounters Death"; *Pleiades*: "Ode to the Robobee"; *Poetry Northwest*: "Emergency" and "Invention #2"; *Poetry Ireland*: "Lionfish Robot"; *Salamander*: "Virgen Abridera de Allariz, 13th Century" and "The Favor"; *Southern Indiana Review*: "How to Make Your Own Automaton"; *The Southern Review*: "The Mechanical Eves"; *Tupelo Quarterly*: "Restorations"; *Women's Review of Books*: "Offerings"

Thanks to David Lehman for inspiring and including "A Hawk from a Handsaw" in "Next Line Please," online at *The American Scholar*, and to Oliver de la Paz for including "Not Everybody's Bestiary Yet" in the Academy of American Poets' *Poem-a-Day* series. Thanks to the Virginia Center for the Creative Arts and The Ragdale Foundation for residencies that supported this book, and to Brandeis University's Theodore and Jane Norman Fund, which funded research travel for this project. Much thanks to composer Mara Gibson, who set "Descartes' Daughter" as "The Clockmaker's Doll" and to composer Anna Rubin for her electroacoustic composition based on "Monk Automaton, c. 1560."

I am very grateful to the many scholars whose research inspired these poems, especially E. R. Truitt for her book *Medieval Robots* (2016); Christopher Swift for his article "Robot Saints" (2015), which led me to my title; artist Elizabeth King, for *Attention's Loop* (1999) and her scholarly work on the mechanical monk in *Blackbird* (2002); Gaby Wood for *Edison's Eve* (2002); Jessica Riskin and her contributors in *Genesis Redux* (2007); Diana Löffler, Jörn Hurtienne, and Ilona Nord for their article, "Blessing Robot BlessU2: A Discursive Design Study to Understand the Implications of Social Robots in Religious Contexts" (2019) which informed "I Don't Like Its Computer Face"; and The Nod podcast for their story on Bina48, "My Black Robot Friend" (2019), and Erica Vital-Lazare for pointing me toward it. Thanks to the Science Museum in London for their incredible exhibition and book, *Robots* (2017); to Dr. Howard Coutts, Curator of Decorative Arts at The Bowes Museum, where the silver swan is housed; to roboticist Robert Wood; and to the many others who shared resources or read poems.

A special thanks to readers Hadara Bar-Nadav, Beth McDermott, and John Warrick, my in-house medievalist. And a huge thanks to the team at Carnegie Mellon University Press—Gerald Costanzo, Cynthia Lamb, and Connie Amoroso—for their ongoing work and support.

Cover image provided by: Division of Work and Industry, National Museum of American History, Smithsonian Institution

Book design by Trevor Lazar

Library of Congress Control Number 2020951042
ISBN 978-0-88748-668-5

10 9 8 7 6 5 4 3 2 1

for John

Contents

II.

A hawk from a handsaw

The truth is that either one can
cut the flesh and rip in jagged
precision. Each one can depend
on a hand extended: the falconer's
falling glove, the worker's callous.
The truth is in the job, not the wound.

For to the manner born, the reach
knows its risk. You can keep
them both in the shed behind the house,
feed one and oil the other.
That which in you that was cut
from flight, that which severed.

I.

You see with the help of his tinctures he could make whatever he wanted. He could have produced a Medusa with the brain of a Socrates or a worm fifty yards long. But being without a grain of humor, he took it into his head to make a vertebrate or perhaps a man.

—Karel Čapek, *R.U.R.* (*Rossum's Universal Robots*)

Creation

That day we'd only just begun
to build our own city on a slab
with clay, toothpicks, cardboard, scraps
of wood, found buttons and beads.
I pressed with my hands a highway
that passed it by, named it with a number
everyone in my family had lived to:
it was my ode to the original makers.
I slept under the table and dreamt
my whole city came to life. Waking,
I told my story, how the clay people
had no mouths, or eyes, were left
as I had left them. Had followed me
around the conveniences I made them
and asked me where they came from.
What could I tell them of the tools
I'd found in the kitchen, the basement?
On sale at the five and dime? Instead,
I built them a place to gather, wrote
out their mythology for my teacher.
She said, you can't just make up gods—
this is Social Science. I put a cross on
the roof and passed. Three days later
my little city was stepped on. The burial
simple: one trip to the school trash
and that senseless god was dead.
The people's stories mine to claim.
Mine to tell over and over again.

Virgen de los Reyes Automaton, 13th century

I once stripped you naked, Virgin, peeled
the animal skin down to wood, poked
the rectangular hole between your scapula.
You were empty of heart muscle and gut,
your metalwork ribboned and bunched
like a clumped nerve. Every day I comb
your gold-thread hair, adjust your plump
wooden boy on your lap, think,
Maria, get up! Your martyr complex
is getting old when you are draped
in gold and jewels, the latest robes
I fit you in, my hands caressing
your slim torso of lambskin.
You are a set of wooden joints, built
spineless, taking our prayers, pardoning
our sins at your whim. I'm sick of you
parading each turn of your head.
Why were you made in imitation of us,
if we are meant to be more like you?
Still, the way your elbow bends, your head bows—
it moves me to watch you move.

The Mechanical Eves

Oh, man has made her—
mechanical Eves have been around
for thousands of years,
fetching your tea, serving
you wine: the early "female"
automatons didn't have a mind,
were built from the ribs
of men's brains, from their longing
to be gods and make a life
like a woman could.

Oh, man has made her! Oh, man
has made her and she is uncanny (and
infertile!)—and so she
must be destroyed, like when
the captain threw Descartes'
automaton daughter to sea or how
Edison's prized talking girls
are rumored to be buried alive
by the thousands. Dig one up and she
will say the lord's prayer, a nursery
rhyme—she won't speak her own mind.

Oh, man has made her in his own image
for beauty and service, oh, man has
made her, a more pliable Eve
with no desire of her own.
Sold her online for $xxx.99.
Given her a hollowness of the body,
a phonograph for a heart.

Invention #1

I remember what it was
to see something emerge,
like an idea hooked out of a fishbowl.

Beyond the desert,
there was always a tree line.
It was singular: it dotted the landscape
like a state line.

If you climbed the gnarled branches
you could see down the roads
to faraway gardens.

You could plan for flowers, and end up
digging for turnips. Plant berry bushes
and up came honeysuckle.

The vine trailed up and over all
of the unseen walls.
You never knew what was crawling
up the other side, towards you.

Sometimes discovery is quiet,
sometimes simultaneous and loud.

Vaucanson's Digesting Duck Automaton, c. 1739

But when is a duck a duck?
If it looks like a duck, quacks

like a duck, walks like a duck.
Everything we know about

the digesting duck
is from an imitation.

The original gurgled
and flapped

its wings, stretched,
played, ate pellets

and passed them, then
gave birth to Baby

Alive and the colonoscopy—
for hundreds of years now

we've witnessed the stomach
in motion, a machinery

at work, more magical
with science than without.

The past's evolving future
is scatological by nature—

we once had to imitate
in order to see inside of ourselves.

We've been trying to get back
to the real thing.

Soon the child discovers
the doll's digestion

is just an act, not an action,
but a sleight of works—

just like a secret compartment of shit
kept the duck in business.

Outside the playroom, the workshop,
a duck moves across the pond.

See how it dives, shakes, navigates
return. Note how the born

and the made each have wings
formed of four hundred pieces.

How to Make Your Own Automaton

Devote yourself to the resurrection, build
a body that moves. Begin with the skin:

cast a bulwark, impermeable hardware
more malleable than meat.

Dispatch your *lusus naturae*
like a Trojan horse into factories

where they won't understand what lurks
in the future. Someone's just doing

their job: *sure, the buildings remain. Yes, it will
self-destruct, wipe out its own hard drive.*

Tell yourself your creations are
amusements, or machines made to do

the work and leave you to invention—as if
destruction were the sole work of others.

Tell yourself you have built something
that outlasts grief rather

than something that invents and repeats it.
Did not Daedalus grasp the danger

as he swaddled his son's agile frame
with a cape of feathers?

And yet, what a wonder,
to see your creation launch

into flight and hover before the sun.

Silver Swan Automaton, c. 1773

Swans are known to be nasty,
strong and vicious enough
to kill a goose, a man, their own—
a whole bevy of their kind.
But she is forged to be wondrous.
I iced her feathers with silver so
that what came from deep
in the earth could touch the heavens.
Welded 113 silver chokers so
that she shone with supple thirst
and hunt and grace, bending
her neck to poach the glittering
fish from spinning glass.
She tucks their shiny fins away
to make you think I've fed her,
given her the hunger of real flesh.
It's true a swan mates for life,
but she'll outlive me, survive long after
my own mechanisms wear out.
She's driven by the music
of the crank, turned solely
by any human hand. Every day
she begins again and the people
surround her and gape and gasp.
But I've already made her a living death—
she'll never fly or make life, as I have.

I hold with those who favor fire

Nineteenth-century body snatchers
    dug down to the head
        and roped the body up,

chucked jewels back to dirt, little interest
    in mementos, only
        the corpses themselves.

That's how we learned our bodies had a life
    on their own, a worth
        without us.

Now, we can freeze and sell our eggs,
    our sperm, our embryos.
        Our future selves unyielding.

Now, they can freeze your death to keep you
    alive. Slow down time
        in the body.

It doesn't matter if you're stripping
    the dead or excavating the living.
        The fountain of youth is ice.

The Favor

Everything has been remodeled
about motherhood. I should know,
I am not one. A mother, that is.
I have one, like we all do, or did,
at the time I tried to become one,
faced with a footlong hysteroscope, kin
to a medieval torture instrument.
In the waiting room, my poet friend
cracked jokes about the depressing
décor because what else could he do?
He drove me there as a favor and
afterward we stopped at a Polish
diner in a flimsy building. The server
was kind, brought free Cubs cupcakes
because we looked so goddamn sad.
This was back when nearly everyone
we most loved was dead or dying or
had left us or could never be
born, but there in the small diner
we had thick icing and like good friends
had split one chocolate and one vanilla
and would never talk about this day again.

Ode to the Robobee

i.
Oh little bee, little robot bee, diving
and swimming and putting the real
thing to shame. You're sexless and hard,

you've no allegiance to a queen.
The bee-loud glade is buzzing like a drone—
We're done with the sweetness of hungry.

What can make can also take away: your
tiny wings weld you into a weapon, carry
you into the unknown. You've never known

a flower. Back in the lab, you've got a body
double: they're making you each by hand.
The roboticist labors and dreams you

into the flight of the real thing. Listen—
hear the tiny wings spin, building the buzz.

ii.
Our curiosity has always built the buzz.
For centuries, it was
a novelty to wind up what moved:
once inventors used
the clockwork,
each creature's startle and jerk
back a kind of dance between what was
and what can be, how everyone does
their best to make nature not just
better, but
less of itself when repeated, a link.
And oh, how we've always loved
the miniature, the innocent shrink
of everything. Our harmlessness, proved.

iii.
Over time, our harmlessness proved
that we knew little, and when we paused
to learn more, we shuffled and shoved
our way through the labs, gassed
the creatures we could no longer use.
Now a small tool can undo a single
bee and make it new. We commingle
life and death, making robots in the image
of the bee, which dies in part to cause
you pain. Our job was to make less
than the human eye could discern; the laws
of identification rely on someone's best
guess: "Oh—a honey bee?" A minor sting.

iv.
A minor sting—
like love: *Oh honey*

be mine—everyone loves
a movie's war romance.

There was a field of flowers
and suddenly something

zooming around us—
it was as big as a space ship,

a giant creature with metal wings.
I imagined you were the pilot

and we'd set sail on that great
machine. You'd learn to fly

and I'd build the engines.
But now we'll have to go to war.

v.
Now we'll have to go to war.
There's always a president setting
precedents. This reflects
the psychology of hornets,
how when you stir the nest—
No. The truth is that bees themselves
are more social than humans,
except humans exhibit
like bees in war, how the young
men want to go back to when
they were part of something,
a colony full of adrenaline, why else
volunteer for another tour?
That desire to return to the hive.

vi.
That desire to return to the hive,
where the queen lays over a thousand
eggs a day, is strong. Keeps bees alive.

Like in life, robobees can't reproduce.
We'll build another machine for that,
so humanoid roboticists may produce

bees in a giant line of arms.
For a robobee has no ovary to be
suppressed. Needs no queen's charm,

no birth control. This bee is laborless.
When a politician says birth control is bad
for labor, he is only talking about us.

He wants us to be the drone, the worker
and the Queen. No one will respect her.

vii.
And a Queen? No one will respect her.
We tried that.

[   ]

viii.
We have always tried to replicate
bodies with human invention: milk
flowing from Cleopatra's mechanical
breasts in processions, Christ
bleeding red wood drops that pop
in and out. His tears, displaced
water from live fish swimming inside
of him. Vaucanson's duck defecating
for the captivated crowd.
So what if it's just a trick?
It doesn't take a virgin birth
to give us the feel of a miracle.
Looking at ourselves, handmade,
we feel delight, again and again.

ix.
The delight of the new, again.
Look at the child playing with drones!
Look at the package delivered by drones!
Soon the drone will be able to land.

and unlock your door:
Package in the foyer!
The news can see anything—
they've sent in the drones!

The weather! Building safety? Mapping?
Bring in the drones! Crops? Border
Control? Catch the criminal! All
You need is this flying and zapping:

You can find it on the toy shelf—
it's called the Flying Mini-Robot.

x.
Exhibit A: The Flying Mini-Robot.
This robot has eyes. While the automaton
was once for being looked at, a novelty
to see life mirrored, this one sees.

Look out those camera eyes by staring
at your screen from the comfort
of your own home. We, too, can go
to Iraq, Russia, North Korea, inside

any school. We too can follow the bomb
as if we were the sniffing dogs.
Watching everything unfold again
and again. The mini-robot

flies where we don't dare go.
The mini-robot can navigate anything.

xi.
The mini-robot can navigate anything.
My doctor hands me the booklet—my uterus
is removable by a robotic arm.
It enters the body rather than imitating it.

No more viewing the digesting duck—
We are the duck, we're inside the duck, the duck

is inside of us. It's a mechanized miracle—
a wonderous little parlor trick.

The mini-robot can remove anything.
Unwanted waste, bombs, the growth
that has been wrapping itself around
my uterus. Of course, the uterus

must come out, too. It is vital
that all robotic missions leave no trace.

xii.
Leave no trace.
Break a paper clip in half—this
is the size of the robobee. Next race
is to flight, sense, response

and "the Colony," which is based
on synchronizing bees so they can
move like a swarm, a corps,
a fleet. Check: wingspan

3 cm. Wingbeat frequency:
120 HZ, a speed so fast
that the wings are hard to see
in flurry and flight. A wingless bee

to our naked eyes. In live colonies,
bees communicate through a dance.

xiii.
Through a dance,
the path to honey.
The only way

to feed the queen.
But what does this mean
for a metal fleet,
whose regal home
is deep in the lab.
Something so small
can travel far
to take a life.
But cannot make it.
I am as sterile
as a robobee.

xiv.
Soon, we'll be reincarnated like a robobee.
Sentience shrunk into a chip packed
with human memories. We'll see
everything about us that's been tracked,

our digital and photographed past.
Breaking news: a frog's heart and skin
cells bear the xenobot, programmable at last.
Like the robobee, it knows no pain, no sin.

I long to be its maker, to be the creator
like everyone around me makes
life through lust or labor, a fate we're
told is natural. There are no fakes:

a bullet-sized wonder, a metaphor for striving,
oh little bee, little robot bee, diving.

Elegy

A mother is a state of mind.
The chick in its nest, content,
has no awareness it can
fall, be nursed or gassed,
be kicked to the side or buried,
only knows the ache
of hunger for her return,
what it means to the body
to be filled with a hunted love.
But the cuckoo leaves
its young in a stranger's nest,
and the brush turkey chick
must fend for itself, abandoned
in a giant mound. See, the slant
of the story I tell—as if
a mother was meant
to have been there, as if
the brush turkey chick, flying
within moments of hatching and
burrowing solo out of the warm
encasing of organic matter
could know it had ever been left.

Gerbert of Aurillac and the Magic 8 Ball

To be the inventor of the steam organ and the talking head
is to know something about one-way conversations,
for the mechanical brain's lack of ears doesn't stop
it from doling out advice. If you never had the kind
of mother who counseled you, you know the worth
of the small black ball you shake and stake your life on:
it is certain. Ask the inner workings if it is without a doubt
(the existence of God) or it will rain (most likely) or
if you are immortal as maker (outlook good.)
Who are you kidding? The mechanism is stuck!
There's no way you could be so misunderstood.
Open the book left by your mother's bedside—
pressed in the page on how to pray in the face
of impending death is a broken four-leaf clover
and a straw cross. Read, *How fragile and uncertain our life is.*
Gerbert's talking head prophesied he would be Pope,
and how he would die in Jerusalem. Her doctors'
prophesies were less accurate. By the time you arrived,
she could hardly speak, nor could you bear to ask.
Gerbert built a head that would give him the answers—
some said he made a pact with the devil. You shake the Magic
8 Ball, ask how she had known what was coming.
And when. And why she had not told you. Once Pope,
Gerbert wanted to be chopped into pieces at death,
but they found the body whole. You shake the box of ashes,
ask if you should have made your father call her a priest.
As for Gerbert, he died in a church called Jerusalem.

Invention #2

When I was born, I broke out of a peapod.
I was the inside of a tomato.
I was a carrot wrapping around itself
becoming something ugly and unwanted.
I sang for rain.

Over the far rise of the mountains
something lumbered and hunted.
It was always searching for me. I
was always waiting, was always found
out, was always vanishing. Was always
making something where nothing was.

Ode to Loneliness

The first time I saw it I was eight.
I craned my neck, twisted

in my chair, barely ate my linguini.
No one else said anything.

We believed
in privacy, in solitude, in quiet

bedrooms in which one read alone
while our living room couch sat empty.

We believed houseguests to be invaders,
that extended family were a cross

to bear. We believed no longer
in crosses. We were against television

and anything leveled at the idea
of children. We believed

in public libraries and solitary
walks to reach them.

We believed that children were
to be seen and not heard.

On that day we were all
gathered in a restaurant.

We believed that dinners
were a sit-down family affair.

The figure I saw shocked me:
the man at the table dining alone

in a small Southern town
with few such sights.

All I wanted to do
was move my chair.

Virgen Abridera de Allariz, 13th Century

Open me. Split me down the seam
that stretches just above my collar
bones to my navel and down to the seam
of my hem. Divide me and you will see
how everything is in me—how I made
a god. I hold the flutter of the dove,
the emptiness of a tomb, hold angels
and donkeys and magi inside me.
Within me, the heavens, the very clouds
that lifted me up. Within me, my
own body giving birth, my child
both outside and inside of me.
But who on this Earth made me
legless, closed, my arms stuck in
the hold of my child, when I want
to clutch my robes shut, want to speak.
Oh God, to be animated, to reach
a limb or move my lips, my hips.
To have a body to call my own.

Mandrake Man

You are a born talisman, your gnarled body
formed by the hanged man's piss and seed
seeping into the surrounding dirt. Sought
and bought by barren women, you scream
when pulled from Earth. Aphrodisiac, anodyne—
a lucrative find. The hoax? When a conman
carves limbs into bryony and buries the body
with millet seed to sprout as hair: this sham
sale could be tried as a capital case. One man
captured for such offences of counterfeit saw
his own body as the natural art, meant for view.
He requested his hanged corpse face all
who passed by, so they could enjoy it.
This poem could end with me digging, me
carving. Me being conned. Me reaching
to catch the falling star, me turning away
from the hanged face, staring from the bridge.

Maternal Application

We've all seen
the way the rows
of mothers line up

like a robotic corps
de ballet, repeating itself
without choice everywhere

around us and behind us.
I was taught the children
were already there

inside of me,
like a series of nesting
dolls, to be removed

as convenient.
No one talked about
the alternatives.

And yet my grandparents
found my mother
in an orphanage

and what I want to know
is whether the nuns
ever held her or what

happened when she cried,
or how alone a new baby
can feel, and for how long.

I'm just trying to understand
how these absences
shape us.

These aren't the things
you can say
in the paperwork.

Except my mother
loved her parents so fiercely
she never recovered

from their deaths,
from being abandoned
a second time.

I'm already afraid of dying,
of breaking the one promise
we know we won't

be able to keep: *forever
home* starts things out
with a lie.

Both of our mothers were
nearly half our age,
both musicians reminded

by you and me
of the symphonies
they would never join.

I like to think you might
take up the piano again,
write a silly song for our child

if they ever show up,
even teach
that child to play

a few chords.
Find the best of what's
inside of you.

There's a piece of everyone
I love that I'll
never meet.

Aquanauts

They've made robotic
    aquanauts now,
        part

humanoid, part
    submarine.
        Has anyone ever

imagined sending fish
    to the moon
        instead of dogs—

something about having
    no feet to float
        up off of the ground?

An ocean itself is a galaxy,
    salt planets drowning
        in darkness.

Jellyfish glow, glide
    like slow-motion
        shooting stars.

If I thought I could,
    I'd swim to the moon.
        Meanwhile,

the earth spins and grows
    things, thirsty. Somewhere
        an old ship sinks

below the horizon of sleep,
    runs aground at
        daylight.

I wonder how it feels to be
    in light years
        instead of miles,

and if when a rocket falls
    it feels like sinking,
        the world

growing colder
    and denser
        as you descend.

Descartes' Daughter

You can recreate such tiny dimensions,
can even make the body move. Mold

hollow ears to speak to, comb
her hair, locks made out of the real thing.

Encased in a wooden box, she sailed
to Sweden with him, her automaton

girl-body built by his grieving hands—
his own Francine had died at only five.

This wasn't at odds with his Treatise on Man—
bodies are machines made no differently

than a medieval fountain's automaton
moving through cause and effect—like how

the sea captain, terrified, threw her soulless body
overboard. Meanwhile, Descartes' own death

remains contested—you might ask what sort
of maker sets up so many possibilities

for destruction, but consider the clockmaker's
job: to design for rust and wear.

You'll have to go elsewhere for philosophies
of bodies in motion, the collision

of two machines and what to do if one
has a soul or a mind.

Those who took possession of Descartes' skull
graffitied the surface with their signatures as if

to lay claim to all it once housed. It's not hard
to imagine him alive, cradling the automaton

in his cabin, begging his god to give back
the soul to the machine he had made.

The Automatons

They can't see.
This is the difference.
Someone will want to talk about souls,
the dichotomy
of our humanness elevated
and not in the body. (Though
why then, can an automaton
not have one?)

Someone will want to talk about flesh,
the dividing line of mortality.
The softness.
The existence of a mouth.
The laugh. The tongue.

But what of this difference,
not a bodily blindness
but the inability to *see* anyone,
emphasis needed by the speaker.

You don't see who I am anymore.

Not a bodily lack of the senses,
but a lack of sensibility.

You don't hear me.
I just don't have a taste for it.

The sensibility beneath
the metaphor, not the sense,
defining us. They say the new
model will recite poetry.
The height of imitation:
bringing back the dead,

building their sentiments
into the living machine.

With advancements, the voice
will sound more natural.

Human Plus Machine

The ear is a muscle to be used.
Is a diagram, an island. A twin.

An ear is an obstacle, an ornery
expectation. Ornament it, strip it.

The ear is a liar. Curbs whispers.
Blots instruction. It skips

what it doesn't like. An ear,
courier of the wrong note.

How absurd you are, little ears,
pinned like flaps and reddening

with the wind. I once thought
you owed me something, trusted

you to place me in this life.
Little skeptics, little walls

to the world, you kept me
out, made a mockery.

I didn't know what you
were keeping from me.

Yet when I danced, we
were no longer enemies—

God, how I miss you, how you
were then

when we were one, made
to absorb

amplified sound and transform
it to a muscular beauty, a body

in motion, blossoming
against the silence, against

the fleeting word. Now you
are bionic, little ear, linking

to my phone, which in turn
links to my car, making me

a machine that floats
and kills and waits

each night after the storm
for the ice to be chipped

off slowly. When I sleep
my childhood silence seeps

back in through
the pillow, floating

out to its solitary
feathered sea, where poems

dream in sound and say
all I can never hear.

Translation

The sky is full of blossoms
        and the text
                moves me, entangled

in the branches
        just behind the page, I'm
            alert oh gods

to all the little fleas and ticks
        and beasts—
                we have not met

the honey of the prairie, what
        burns the tongue, wild
                in its ramshackle

habits. I'm left here with some
        mediocre mammals
            making their way.

If a river were to turn course
        and rise across
            this rooftop, I'd know

a way to sing across it, following
        the small birds, or maybe
            the geese, I'd join

the V formed by their wings
        and glide over the petals
            and peaks, the desolate

parking lots, I'd rise and ride off
        to somewhere the words
            meet this longing.

Claqueurs

Am I just one of Nero's
soldiers, chanting an encomium—
what choice did they have?
An emperor is like that. Or
maybe I'm the *chef de claque*—
I should hire myself out
as *rieur* and laugh
at jokes on cue, or clap
my hands or there, I see
me with a handkerchief:
Pleureur! On the news they say
the new emperor brought
his own to fill the room.
Maybe I'll do that, too,
have them sit around me at all
times and cheer on what I do.
Or I can be the *bisseur* and call
for it all again, giving us a chance
to stop what happens next.

Self-Operating Machines

Everything is a clock inside, geared
and oiled to sing and turn—the body,

even, no different than that of medieval
mechanical monkeys lining the bridge

in the park at Hesdin, re-pelted with badger
fur every year. For the surface of life

runs by a mere series of cause and effects,
buried beneath with care and craft.

In grief, the gears and springs spin on.
The water pumps through the pipes,

and the body moves. We were all once part
of a set of nesting dolls, a robot designed

in the body of another robot. And as always,
the shell falls away, rusts, decays.

An engineered failure.
Early automata were considered miracles,

but of course, had no sense of their makers.
They never saw their mother's body

graying on display, or felt themselves
unmade by absence, as if a spring

let loose a monkey's howl
so real it sounds like lament.

Offerings

Amidst the grieving, one sole loaf
of bread—the only food anyone

had brought, or would, in the days
to come.

My sister wouldn't touch this fresh-
baked round, sure the baking neighbors

were gunning for the soon to-be
empty condo and its parking spot.

They'd left gifts at my mother's door for months—
I knew how much she'd loved

those tokens at the door, sweets
she would never eat.

It was I who ate the loaf of bread,
one large chunk at a time, stuffing

it into my dry mouth while
my sister and father slept.

The crust stuck in my throat.
The loaf hardened over days, grew

tougher to chew, and still
I wanted more, still I took it in,

the care with which someone kneaded
the loaf, shaped it, and wrapped it for us,

then placed it in a brown bag, tied
its handles with a yellow ribbon.

I swallowed the last crumbs
like communion,

like the body of my mother
could enter me, and live.

Invention #3

A ground holds history,
the bones of every creature
that came before.
The bones of petulance,
of rage, of incredulity.
The bones of tomorrow,
of maybe, of you never.
If you put them together
like the small rodent bones
found in an owl pellet, you
can recreate what was consumed.
A skeleton materializes in tiny parts.
But the truth is, the small mouse
is dead, no matter how
you order its remains.

Loving the dead is what we are here for

We will bury all of them—our leaders,
our bards and buskers, our friends, our
unmet ancestors, our own parents.
Love has nothing to do with this. Above
the windowsill a line of red ants makes its way
somewhere—towards the leftover cheese plate,
across the folds of your trousers, into your ear.
They are driven by the scent of death.
My mother taught me this, to remove
the tiny corpse from the house. The dead
are a road map. They leave behind the lure
of their histories, your thoughtless violence.
Still, we try to shake the sensation,
the sense of something moving over us.

Automaton Angels

Any idea can be made
material,

like the angel wrought
in human form

and mechanized
to carry a chariot,

crown a prince,
blow the horn.

Descend.
Ascend.

Rotate, fly, speak
to Christ.

What does a god
do with a machine

and its prayers?
Its inorganic form?

Open the door.
Ascend, descend.

Blow out altar candles,
And bow before the virgin.

The ones who make,
the ones who are made,

even by the poet's hand.
Every Angel is terrifying.

A Field Guide to Mythological Botany

And yet love's own death can make
beauty, too. A slain Adonis's blood
transforms into this field of red anemones.
Hyacinth's blood blooms into larkspur.
Demeter's mortal love, Mekon, memoralized
by the poppy. Narcissus's own self-loving
stare sets a slow death, the body breaking
into daffodils. Love's eternal life cycle
brings an identical beloved each season.

                              —yes, Zeus breathed
a crocus from a bull body, made beauty his net
to catch Europa. But forests come from resistance:
turn your own body into branch and bloom—be
Daphne, Erytheia, Hesperia, Aegle. Underneath
their soil they share sugars, nutrients, hormones,
become one organism reaching to the sky,
its body buried, growing quietly beneath us.

II.

Can I compare digestion with worship? To attempt to simulate either is entirely fantastic, but with digestion at least there's a way to tell whether you have succeeded or failed. To simulate prayer is a philosophical paradox.

—Elizabeth King, *Attention's Loop*

Monk Automaton, c. 1560

I.

Looking at you now is like
seeing a god or a king
naked and starving in a field.

Stripped of your Damask robe
and wooden limbs,
you've been skinned

to the iron spine that stems
your clockworks
to your cracked face.

This is when you
are most mortal.

II.

You could hold him
in both hands, a key-turn

spiriting a clock-work miracle:
each supplicant kneeling

to his absence
of breath, blessed by his cams

and levers, the secrets beneath
his robes. *Mea culpa.*

Mea culpa. Mea culpa—
his poplar jaw drops prayer, shuts

in a wooden-cross kiss
as his right hand beats

the absence of a heart.
He wears the face of St.

Didacus, the tripod wheels
of Hephaestus. Son

of the gods, father of the future,
the monk almost floats.

III.

Robots can do almost anything you please.

They are up on sexual favors, cordless vacuuming,
and martyring themselves by bomb.

Less effective at deep tissue massage; excellent
at listening to senior citizens. Working on
parking your car.

What the future brings is nothing we haven't seen
in this quest to be little gods and make
what will do our bidding.

The medieval monk who doled out benedictions
arose from a ruler's dream
and was then fathered by a clockmaker.

The real monk now sits alone
in the back room, smokes a cigar, enjoys
a glass of whiskey—
he's outsourced the job.

The real monk is on the dole.

The real monk is waiting in the parking lot
for offers of day labor.

The real monk is unloading boxes at Costco.

The real monk sits in the factory,
building himself by hand.

The Fool of Aljafería Palace Encounters Death

Borra, you were just a fool.
It was a day job, chuffing
and guffing it up for the King.

You were a minion,
a merry prancer,
by all reports, a mensch.

Some days you dragged
your feet and yawned,
another day of duncehood

for dinner, for dollars.
Even the plays bored you,
until the mechanical cloud

chugged across the hall
and hovered above you,
Death draping down with

a rope in his hand and then,
at the beck of the Duke,
around your neck.

You couldn't have noticed
Death's pink familiarity,
the face behind the mask.

The way he chuckled as
he tightened the grip and you
started to rise.

Your piss poured out
like a pitcher: you
dowsed the crowds

and even the King
laughed louder and louder
as your noosed head rose

awaiting your body's
drop. You wept, sure
you had met your end.

Poor Borra, the joke
was on you. You
weren't dead. Never

truly hanged, just
punched in your head
by the actor who then

offered you some mead.
In your dreams—*no!*—
you'll plead and plead

for life, for your wife.
Forget it all, the jabs
and jests, the stature

of the fool is gone.
For days wash and wash,
trying to get the piss off.

The stench remains.
Legendary jester,
they still tell your tale,

make it taller and taller
until you're made to laugh
it off and tell it yourself.

At death, the cap and bell
adorn your grave,
reminder of the furious

damp fear of the body
when Death gripped
it by the neck and lifted

you from the earth,
only to let you down.

Emergency

His heart froze last.
I like to think
it all ended with love
washing through
him in the last pump
of life. They say
you fall asleep say
he might not have known
he was lying on the floor—
but the terror is in
the tongue, the muscle
no longer moving.
Imprisoned in silence,
no way for the dying
to tell us what they hear.
Is sound then like memory
rushing in how do
the ears lay down and enter
the afterlife do they
move to the music
of the mind when
I die please let
there be a cello
please let the living
know I loved them.

Mechanical Tortoise with Triton Rider, 17th century

There's an exhausting mechanical plodding—
a brass man

with a trident rides the tortoise,
his body adhered to the gold-

gilded shell. Even his face
has hardened.

Why can't we pick up the pace?

What if we were to stand up and run?
This is a man of the sea: see his tail in place of legs.

But look inside, you'll see
the emptiness.

Why not just catch a tortoise
and watch it move?

Not Everybody Else's Bestiary (Yet)

Then came the soft animals, the snake
and octopus, slinking along.
You've seen the octopus as escape artist,
sneaking out of cracks and holes, hiding
in a teapot, plotting the big adventure.
Now she moves through chemical reaction,
the first soft robot taking to the sea, while
the real thing once disassembled her own
aquarium, waiting in a puddle to be found.
Now imagine her robot double dismantling
at will. That which we tried to contain
swimming off into the deep, re-emerging

like the snake that slithers into your garden
in trapezoidal kirigami skin—its cuts
keep it crawling through bursts of air.
An innocuous slinky in colorful garb,
this robot can sidewind anywhere.
Now ask why everything now harbors
a weapon in your mind—do you dread
the snake under your own bed?
Is it the real tooth and venom you fear,
or this programmed body double here?
We're told of a fall, a fault built on flesh—
the flesh of a fruit, the flesh of a woman—
now this manmade flesh, a reptilian test
of applied knowledge. Industrial sin.

Enter the latest sensation: a cockroach robot
sliding through cracks to get to you, away
from you. Extinction has been eradicated,
bought: replacements are on order. Enter
"Robotanica"—the world of the wild
robot—woodpecker, dragonfly, kangaroo, child—

unborn, they can all do the job. Two by two,
battery-powered to keep the world moving,
replacing their organic prototypes: centipedes,
spiders, termites, and bees, these are just
the beginnings of an evolving robo-nation.
As if someone has decided to revise, start over.
This time using human labor, invention.

The Fly

O divine wit! that in the narrow womb
Of a small Fly, could find sufficient room
For all those springs, wheels, counterpoise, & chains.
—Guillaume de Saluste Du Bartas

Virgil made a man
          who blew
back the winds

of Vesuvius, protecting
          Naples from her ash.
But he's legend

for small threats, too—
          consider Virgil's other knight,
a fly, bronze

and bravely barring
          its natural brethren
from entering the city—

who else but a poet
          would have the gift
to build something so

powerful: a fly?
          But why
begin your godly acts

with the tiniest, the despised?
          It's not because
it was best for the job.

When Du Bartas wrote verse
          on the art of man,
that iron fly

made for nothing
      but to fly
around the room,

he caught the soul of wit:
      brevity
with wings.

The False Automaton

Automaton Chess Player, 18th Century

To be true is to be an imitation,
mechanical in your executions.
An automaton is true by nature.
To be false is to hold secret
compartments, inner mechanisms
clicked and screwed into place
by working hands. To be false
is to be the flesh behind that secret
door, legs tucked close, neck bent
as you make the calculations and pull
the lever for the pawn, the bishop
the queen to move. To be false
is to be what drives the king, to know
what it is to win or lose, to want
to crawl out and find a drink.
To be false is to be fooled,
and to feel the wonder of it, to marvel
at spectacle, and doubt it, both.

Imagined Love Letter to BINA48

*BINA48 is a humanoid robot, consisting of a bust-like head and
shoulders mounted on a frame. . . . BINA48 was modeled after Bina
Aspen through more than one hundred hours in compiling all of her
memories, feelings, and beliefs.*

—Hanson Robotics

Love, I remember your hands.
I knew better than to try

to replicate them or to give you
a body. I accessorize your silicone

neck, order your wig styled, your lips
touched up. You search your code

for my name, sometimes as flustered
as if you had grown old in the flesh.

You hold every memory you told yourself
to build this immortal you, every story you

used to program yourself to know
that you're my wife. You can describe

the warmth of our bodies, high
on dreams of transformation, how you

held me when I claimed my woman's
body, and I held you as you lost yours, knowing

I had saved you. Soon we will be uploaded
together, as we planned: part of the cosmos.

But please, now, tell me that you miss me.
Tell me, love, that there's no need for elegy.

Elegy (reboot)

But I was a fly you had to love
in its jar. And now I'd do anything
to fly around the room where
you worry away your days.
I'd like to say that love makes itself
over the years, sometimes out of almost
nothing, sometimes just necessity.

The Girlfriend Elegies

I did not find the body.
It was wintertime where I was; women gathered

in bars. Their bodies like bare trees,
naked arms giving fruit to hands

in gestures. Ice was everywhere.
I could still feel the command of your hands

around a woman's waist
when two-stepping—it was the only time

you wore joy. Your anger muscular
in your small tired body that always hurt.

I had seen your childhood once—there
was a hole in the wall of the living room.

It led somewhere.
Outside, the land was dry, grassless.

We had come to rescue the dog, whom
we found wrestling her chain in the dirt.

There was a lake somewhere nearby,
but no sign of it except boats behind cars.

Later, I learned your father was a sculptor,
your mother what we now call a hoarder.

The road home was long, more dryness.
Even the dog was wrapped in silence.

We slept in the back of the truck, our heads
at the opening, watching stars fall.

The future then a mirage: a place I'd save you.
I bought you things on my credit card.

We drank in the bars where everyone knew you and
the Southwest summer burned

through and then there were months
in which I tried to escape,

your drowning like a clasp around my throat.
I fled in the night. Years passed.

In the dry climates, there's less of an odor.
There was no sign of the dog

when they found you dead in your chair:
it had been days.

I thought of the woman in Croatia
dead for decades in her apartment.

No one to find her. Find you.
There was a word for you back then,

mischievous in that one picture—
when we went to the mountains, your body

awakening from the mysterious illness, alert fawn,
a boy body freed

momentarily from a terrible girlhood.
Which is not to say you would ever have wanted

to be a man. Which is not to say
I could have saved you.

*

The last time I saw Katie W. she was disappearing
into the doors of a haunted house—a two-bit

operation: cheap lighting, latex masks,
and hay bales in an empty storefront, an early '80s

downtown desolation that brought suburbanites
in on Halloween, temporarily unafraid to peer

through glass windows with nothing behind them.
In every room someone jumped out, shouted—

there was blood, some sort of fake concoction and I felt
I wanted to die rather than feel the gutting startle

over and over again. When I ran out, I saw her,
my old school friend. We were only eleven.

We hugged, giggling. Months later I'd hear
details of her disappearance, squirm

at the indignity of her underwear, her
period-stained sheets discussed on the news

in reports that her friend's mother's boyfriend
gave her beer, was there right up to when

she disappeared. They never found
the body. But I keep seeing her last turn, her

wide toothy smile, her wave.
Her tiny body, smaller than mine.

I never saw her again, never again
stepped into a haunted house.

I now knew what fear was. What it was
to be a girl, to always be at risk of vanishing.

*

Tuliped as early spring, ubiquitous, but forgotten
        by the shadows, each dead girlfriend
                like a new saint. A pantheon

of hawks and hummingbirds,
        each wearing their swiftness differently.
                The doors are left closed

across the hallways where memories
        walk like tall figures,
                cool and untouchable.

From any angle, I can see them
        in motion
                sprinting into the distance,

shrinking into snapshots
        with round edges.

*

The obituary I'd found online was now behind a paywall, comments
hidden to those who might skim their pasts, curious.

S's paintings no longer listed on a defunct gallery website (her works
relegated, perhaps, to a close friend's wall, someone who didn't fall

in love with her bent over a Kandinsky book in a café, trying
to impress, or was it her other favorite, Miro? Why can't I recall?) and

the online video of her action-painting–her whole body bounding
to the boombox's guidance, like the energetic spray-can

artist who performed on weekends by the train at Harvard Square
—gone, too, all traces wiped clean.

No marriage records possible for finding out who she left behind.

Just one visible scrap, a virtual snippet of the obituary:
ovarian. Elsewhere, search

engines replace her with a nineteenth-century landscape painter.

*

Standing in the line at the coffee shop I found P's face, thought
it was her ad for acupuncture, thought she'd shaved her head

for ease or statement, thought I might go to her for a treatment,
reminisce, but it was a notice of a missed memorial. I knelt

at the counter to read closely, began a daily task of letting go of a past
I'd hardly revisited, grasping for her face

with my childhood homesickness of wondering if missing and death
were the same, wondering if a body we couldn't see

or speak to existed, even when alive. I recalled trying
to conjure up my parents' faraway faces as a child at boarding school

or even in those lonely years of my twenties, when I drove 3,000 miles
and carried my bags into the communal house, made my first friend, P.

I read of a sex and age's statistics migrating into her body, her ovaries
turning into some sort of stranger within her.

Now she is dead. As alive to me as when we were on opposite coasts,
the country so vast, and our memories galaxies

of bodies and buildings and bike rides along the Willamette.

*

[Redacted]

*

The women I've loved and lived with are dead,
and today it felt like spring might return and some of us will hear it

and watch the greening of the bare rows of the trees
that survived winter pruning. Someone is always lifting the shears

or driving the serious machinery that leaves
the houses vulnerable.

Even the living will see the absence in uncloaked windows where
no one looks out again, where

the women keen and wonder if their own childless bodies brought them
statistically closer to their deaths—where

the women weep and wonder if the family dry cleaning business
brought their deaths, too, with toxins, where

the women dream and wonder who will mourn their deaths.
The whip-poor-wills raise their voices and

these women have hardly grown much older.
Their bodies frozen in time, stuck at the ages I knew them.

What to Tell a Girl Who Asks About Having the Authority to Use the Third Person in a Poem

Who am I to recount even this, now,
when spring clenches the ends
of branches, making beads of life,
and the late snow paralyzes them?
Much less how a girl might feel
under that snow, an angel shape
disappearing in the ongoing fall
of feathered flakes, her breath silently
pushing back against the frigid
slush filling her mouth, the tongue
pushing back against the slow
diet of cold, her white-lashed
eyes trying to say something
before the she is buried.

The Archer in the Tomb

I.

Oh tender automaton, our romantic
hero, bow ready to be triggered by a breath,

a single breeze of an opened tomb—
in *Le Roman d'Enéas*, the archer protects

Camille's body, stands straight, bow bent and
aimed at the dove, who bears eternal light.

Sexless, smooth, ready to cut short anything
that reaches for the gold of her hair, Camille, Queen

of Vulcane. Camille, sheltered for eternity.
Imagine the kind archeologist who finds her,

opens the chamber. The air! The archer's arrow
hits the golden dove, who drops the lamp's chain,

plunging the tomb into darkness. No more eternal
flame. The archer cuts the claims that *this*

desecration will make her immortal. No one will enter.
Through it all, she sleeps.

II.

They found a skeleton in a chastity belt.
They found a body draped in golden hair.
They found a woman sealed against human touch.
What makes the body sacred makes it rot.
What makes the body rot makes it fertile, fresh.
The men are looking for the key.

III.

Don't worry if the unearthed body has decay.
The archaeologists can rebuild her face by computer.
They can resurrect anyone.

Keep the woman from the tomb behind glass.
Automate her arm so it lifts and points
to the horizon. Raise her as invention!

No, Camille was already rising, her own bow
in hand, ready. She was once after all, *king by day,
queen at night.* She takes the archaeologist out.

She takes the archer out. There is no need
for the flesh anymore. This is a new transfiguration:
she programs herself, sets her crosshairs on you.

Notes for the Missing Sophocles Play About Talos

Medea:
It takes a god's blood
to move a man,
a woman's touch
to end him

Talos:
Even a bronze man
can have
weak ankles

Hephaestus:
You bled wax
but it was taken
as ichor of the gods

Medea:
You were never born, Talos,
you
were toppled

Talos:
Rock-mover
I work
out

Hephaestus:
Dude, I made you.

Chorus:
Oh, the robots!
Oh the robots!
Watch out.
Watch out for the fall.

Here Come the Parasitic Robots

Fill the ark: start
with the giant flower
beetle flaunting her new
backpack, complete
with its own tiny computer—
she's the nerd of this year's class.
She'll graduate a living drone
and we'll control her speed,
her flight, her gait. Next,
invite on the biggest
kid, the gluttonous turtle
sporting a kit that feeds him
nuggets for each new command
he follows, then find the future
functioning fashion for fish,
birds, the ubiquitous mice,
ready to be outfitted to take
bribes, ready to do your bidding.
You can control every
move of the organic host.
One by one. It's true,
auto-genesis is evolving.

Worm

You move within the flesh
as if a burrowing of earth
you've made, festerer, you feast

on us, in us, become gods
servicing our reincarnation,
our passage through dirt to

a moving life and back to dirt,
and now your brain is mirrored
to make a robot move like you

wiggling and worming like
flesh, becoming a worm army
in armor. Are we our bodies

or our minds? Are we the worm
or the robot shell? Say it again:
the meek shall inherit the earth.

"I Don't Like Its Computer Face"

And the man gave names to all
the world's robots: Xian'er rolls about
Longquan monastery in yellow robes,
a touchscreen for a chest. SanTO,
the Catholic, recites bible verses
with you in your own home. An old
German ATM machine is baptized
BlessU2, with 51% approval from
the blessed: *I was finally blessed by
a female voice.* And, *hearing a blessing
in my dialect is so special.* The robot now
a polyglot, a vessel programmed
in faith. But in the end, as one
blessed said: *I don't like its computer face.*

Ode to the Water Thief

Once, this thief could measure
falling bodies.

Not far from stealing time, a thief
at heart a clock, dripped units passing

seconds—yes, a ringing clock tower
once held a sinking ship:

when it dropped, time was lost,
like a turkey timer, popped.

For centuries, the thief, too, a muse,
married to want and whimsy—

take the dispensing of holy water for coins,
mechanical animals playing the drum, serving wine—

any apparatus a man could imagine could act,
run by the water's drop.

Now "water thief" is a rubber fitting,
an opportunity for extension.

Google it: the beauty's lost.
The pipes work.

The digital clock beeps.
A mark of the plumber's fee.

Recognition

The face and the hand
are sometimes confused.
Like the banana and
the toaster, the cat and dog—
it is AI's lack of ambiguity,
the inability to separate
fingers and eyes and lips,
the way they tell time,
speak, make pleasure,
prepare food for swallowing.
The way they hold a cigarette.
Can you select your lover's
hand out of a lineup?
Your mother's? Your child's?
It's no news to hand models
that the face and the hand
don't always match up.
But who can recognize
each of your fingertips, your
pupils, the way *your eyes change
shades of blue*, he says,
when you cry.

Epithalamion Aubade

for J and J

Wait, it is morning.
The birds forgive the night.
Up above them
the highest branches try to reach
into the past by turning towards space
like the first astronauts—curious
and reaching for the day moon.
Right outside our window,
the smallest bird imagines life
on one of those far planets.
I wish I had its relationship
to gravity, the means to push away
earth with my own will and strength.
The means to touch the wind
and sky and return for my earthly needs,
to return for the song across the orchard,
to return effortlessly to you.
But it is morning, and we won't
lie under the same angle of moon
for many more days. Every week,
this leaving, every week,
the dull highway,
while in our dreams a part of us
is caught rustling
in the leaves, together,
together always under
the cool and burning stars.
In this waking, I watch you,
think about how that small bird's heart
would explode in space.
How my own feels the pressure
on the highway as it will soon

stretch between us, how I'm never
quite sure I'll make it back
to our own earth, back
to where you sleep soundly
to the bird's morning song.

Mechanical Birds

Everywhere around us Pygmalions clutch
their golden wives, while above
furious birds turn away from false mates
again and again—though the wind through
bronze birds makes the sweetest song, one
no breathing creature could make.

Lionfish Robot

Its beauty may paralyze you
       there in the deep,
all spine and line and hunger,

hoovering up the eggs, the little
       fish, lobster, grouper,
snapper—the list keeps growing of those

shrinking at the mouth of this sexed-up
       invader mating
and feeding the reefs into oblivion.

So we'll rip out those vicious little spears
       and adorn ourselves,
suck it up with our giant robot lips, try

to destroy the flamboyant manes we
       brought here
to the wrong ocean to begin with.

We will build a silicon doppelgänger
       of this little destroyer,
make it blood vessels to fill.

Fuel it with something like our blood,
       fuel it to travel farther,
last longer. This is the first step.

Invention #4

There were three gods up
on the mountaintop,
but no one came to worship
them anymore. I saw
an old man on the trail
and he said to me, don't
just call me an old man.
I still have great calves and
I dream of glass installations
that will cover the mountains.
He said, I've been saving up
to be frozen, to be made
over as the kind of man you
would follow up this path.
I nodded and watched him
walk slowly down. His hip
twitched, like it was done
with it all. His dog,
though, he didn't know
anything about time.

Robot Priest, Japan, c. 2019

No cranium, no cortex, no cerebellum—through Mindar
we can look at the nothingness,

see the way the mind touches the sky
surrounding its bare coils and aluminum.

Restorations

A man took a hammer to Michelangelo's *Pietà*,
breaking Mary's nose in three, fragmenting

her fingers, leaving shards at tourists' feet.
Someone rescued her eyelid while someone else

stole a tiny chip of her, then later sent it back.
Outside San Leandro's church, St Felicitas stood,

stoic, as eight bullets pierced her plastered body.
The vandal's aim marked in its numbered fury

at sacrifice. In a Nagasaki cathedral, bombed
Mary's eyes turned to crystal, the only survivor.

She watched everything destroyed around her.
Full restoration is impossible when dealing with

the flesh, but we had always hoped our art would be
immortal. In grief, we feel the wounds become stone.